SCOUSE ENGLISH

Abson Books London
First published December 2001
11th impression 2011
Cover design Chris Bird
Cover photograph from Rex Features

Printed by Gutenberg Press, Malta
ISBN 9 780902 920941

SCOUSE ENGLISH

compiled by Fred Fazakerley

**ABSON
BOOKS
LONDON**
5 Sidney Square London E1 2EY
Tel 020 7790 4737 Fax 020 7790 7346
email absonbooks@aol.com

PREFACE

Scouse, with its quick repartee and colourful choice of words, reflects the character of its speakers far more accurately than any other dialect of the British Isles. History gave Scousers their tough upbringing, their distrust of authority and an attitude variously described from "embattled alienation" to "truculent paranoia" – and they give voice to this in their speech.

No other British dialect is so well known, both nationwide and overseas, owing to a unique combination of events over the past 50 years. Scouse was almost unheard outside Liverpool until it was brought to the nation's wartime and early post-war ears through radio by comedians Tommy Handley, Arthur Askey and Ted Ray. Television has fed us an endless procession of Scouse comedians, notably Ken Dodd ("waair's me shaaairt?"), Jimmy Tarbuck, Stan Boardman and, more recently, Craig Charles. When The Beatles took the music business by storm, their speech was heard worldwide. In the 1970s, television situation comedies such as The Liver Birds continued this exposure. The Thatcher years brought even more scousers to our screens, through soaps and sitcoms such as Brookside and Bread. Local writers Alan Bleasdale, Carla Lane, Jimmy McGovern and Willy Russell dug deeply into the Liverpool psyche to produce TV plays and films about what it was like to live in 1980s Merseyside. They did not always produce work that was complimentary. Who could forget Bleasdale's Boys from the Blackstuff, with its lead character, the self-destructive Yosser "Gissa job" Hughes? Finally, the exposure of local politicians to national gaze did not bring universal approval of their comments.

The word 'Scouse' has three meanings: a stew, made from cheap cuts of meat and the staple diet of the Liverpool working class; a native of Liverpool; a dialect spoken by the inhabitants of Liverpool.

The meal "Scouse", or "Lob-Scouse" to give it its proper name, was a potato stew containing onions, carrots and meat – usually the cheaper cuts of beef, mutton neck or corned beef. It was an affordable and popular meal for those on low wages (i.e. most of them), eventually giving its name to those eating it and to the way they spoke.

The 19th century saw a huge influx of people into Liverpool from all parts of England, Scotland, Wales and especially Ireland, bringing with it a rich mixture of regional accents, which gave birth to the unique Scouse dialect we hear today.

Formerly confined to Liverpool, Tranmere and Birkenhead, Scouse was rarely encountered, except by visitors to the city. Since the slum clearance and urban redevelopment programmes of the 1950s, with its forced relocation of Scouse speakers in Speke, Kirkby and Skelmersdale, plus a voluntary resettlement in owner-occupied housing estates across South West Lancashire, there is more frequent contact with the Scouse dialect. Hopefully this volume will assist in the understanding of it.

Fred Fazakerley

CONTENTS

A

aah-eh	not fair!	
ace!	well done!; also a noun, e.g. *all right ace*	
ackers	cash	
ahr	our, e.g. *ahr kid*	
allus	always	
arrers	darts	
arse	homosexual, also arse-bandit	
axe	ask, e.g. *dunno, don't axe me*	

B

bags	lots	
bail out	leave	
barney	argument	
bells	o'clock, e.g. *see you at seven bells*	
bender	(i) prolonged drinking session	
	(ii) suspended jail sentence	

bent	stolen property, disreputable
berd	girl, woman
bevvy	alcoholic drink, usually beer
bevvied	drunk
bewk	book
bezzie	best mate
bezzies	best clothes
biddy	old woman
bifta	cigarette
binnie	household refuse collector
bint	see berd
bizzie	police officer
blind	not the slightest, e.g. *he never took a blind bit of notice*

blind scouse	meatless stew (see Scouse)
blitzed	drunk
blow	take a break from work
bluey	five pound note (see Flim)
bobbin	unauthorised time off work
boss!	marvellous!
Bootle buck	hard-faced biddy
boozer	pub
box	(i) vagina
	(ii) mental, e.g. *off his box*
boxed	pregnant
brassic	penniless
buggeroo	naughty boy
butty	sandwich

C

cat	goalkeeper, e.g. *top cat* = good goalkeeper
can't half	really good, e.g. *can't half play footy*
catlick	(i) Roman Catholic
	(ii) a light wash
chemicked	drunk
chippy	fish and chip shop
chokka	full
choss	chaos
chuck	(i) food
	(ii) throw; and, occasionally, the equivalent of the nearby Lancashire term of endearment, 'luv'
chuffed	happy
ciggie	cigarette
clever	healthy, e.g. *I'm not feelin' too clever*

college pud	student	
cop shop	police station (there really is one with that name in the city centre)	
corpy	Liverpool City Council	
cozzie	swimsuit	
crack	good time	
cracker!	great!	
crack on	recognise	
creased	tired	
Crimbo	Christmas	

D

dairty	filthy
dale	they will, e.g. *dale do dat*
damage	cost, price

darrel	that will, e.g. *darrel do*
dat	that
dead	very, e.g. *dead 'andy* = convenient, *dead 'andsome* = good-looking, *dead ringer/dead spit* = exactly alike
dekko	look
dem	those
dick	detective (now obsolete)
diddy	small (immortalised as the Diddymen, companions of Ken Dodd)
dig out	clean, e.g. *gotta dig out me gaff*
divvy	stupid
do one	run away
doddle	(i) easy, e.g. *it's a doddle* (ii) that will do, e.g. *doddle do okay*

dodgy	(i) risky
	(ii) suspect goods
doins	(see thingy)
doll	girl, woman (almost obsolete)
dolled up	overdressed
done up	overdressed
dozey	stupid
duff	(i) defective, e.g. *a duff telly*
	(ii) pregnant, e.g. *I'm up the duff, doctor*
dur	there
dursent	dare not

ere!	excuse me!
eorta	he really should…

F	**feller**	husband (originally, but now can be a male companion of any description)
	fetch	bring
	filth	police
	flim	five pound note
	footy	football
	frisby	lesbian
G	**gaff**	home, house, residence
	gaffer	boss, foreman (semi-obsolete)
	gaffless	homeless
	gear!	marvellous!
	gear	illegal drugs
	ghost	accompanying a workmate and watching him work, but doing nothing oneself

gimme	give me, e.g. *gimme a ciggy*
gissa	e.g. *gissa job* (see gimme)
gob	(i) mouth
	(ii) to spit
goolies	testicles
goosegog	gooseberry
gorra	got a, e.g. *gorra ciggy?*
gorrany	do you have any, e.g. *gorrany ciggies?*
gorrup	overdressed
goosed	exhausted
gozzie	(i) squinty eyes
	(ii) contraceptives
graft	work
grass	inform, informer
grotty	squalid

| **H** | **hold on!** | wait a moment! |
| | **hooter** | nose |

| **I** | **iddle** | it will, e.g. *iddle do dat* |

J	**jack**	detective (now obsolete)
	jar	glass of beer
	jarg	fake designer clothes
	jerry	chamber pot
	jew	do you, e.g. *jew wanna ciggie?*
	jigger	back alley
	judy	girl, woman (semi-obsolete)
	jockey	driver

K

kaylied	drunk
kid	brother (usually the younger one, but sometimes it can be the older brother and, occasionally, the sister)
kidda	more affectionate term for the above
Kirkby kiss	headbutt

L

la	lad, e.g. *alright la?*
la la	Scouser with a pronounced accent
lamp	(i) strike hard
	(ii) surreptitiously watch
lanny	Mersey ferry landing stage
lavvy	toilet
lecky	electricity, e.g. *lecky man* = meter reader, *lecky board* = electricity company

left-footer	Roman Catholic
lemme	permit me
lennus	loan me
lezzie	lesbian
like	equivalent of "you know"
loosie	the odd cigarette
lorra	large amount, e.g. *gorra lorra money*
lushed	hopelessly drunk

M

made up	pleased
mam	mother
mate	sir (this has now replaced the obsolete 'wack', 'wacker', 'tosh' and 'mush' as a greeting)

marmalise	beat up
mennal	insane
merry	slightly drunk
miladdo!	my old friend! (not always spoken in a friendly tone)
milkie	milkman
mingy	mean, stingy
mitts	hands
mobie	mobile 'phone
moggy	cat (none of the controversy over this word which has so divided Lancashire)
mouth!	you're talking too much!
mush	mate (now obsolete)

N

nan	grandmother (sometimes pronounced 'nin')
nick	versatile noun or verb, meaning:
	(i) arrest
	(ii) steal
	(iii) prison
	(iv) police station
nicker	pound
Nitty Nora	school nurse
nits	lice
nix	nothing
nouse	intelligence
nut	see Kirkby kiss
nuts	testicles
nutt'n	nothing

O

oavy	overtime
on top!	out of order!
oodles	large amount
oojah	(see thingy)
outer	out of, e.g. *outer work*
owl	older person, e.g. *owl feller* = father, *owl girl* = mother
ozzy	hospital

P

pairm	hairdo
palatick	helplessly drunk
petty	toilet (originally outside)
Prod	Protestant (plural: Proddies)

Q

queen   term of endearment for female

queenie   homosexual

queer   stranger; only just recognised, e.g. *who's that queer feller*? Strong Irish ("quare") influence

R

redneck   Roman Catholic

rennie   rent collector

rob   steal

rozzer   policeman (now obsolete)

ropy   doubtful quality

rotten   very drunk

runs   diarrhoea

S

sanny	environmental health inspector
sarney	sandwich
scally	rogue (in the sense of loveable rogue)
scarper	run away
Scouse	(i) type of meat stew
	(ii) dialect spoken in Liverpool
	(iii) inhabitant of Liverpool
Scouser	alternative for (iii) above
scoff	food
scram	food
scuffer	policeman (now obsolete)
screw	burgle
shirtlifter	homosexual
short-arse	small

shtum!	shut up!
shop	(see grass)
sit off	do nothing
skinny	(see mingy)
skinny ma link	thin
skint	(see brassic)
slog	work, e.g. *hard slog 'ere mate*
slummie	small change
smart	good health
sniff	inform on welfare cheats
snitch	steal
sock robber	person from a disreputable district
soft ollie	stupid
sowsh	social security
sound!	excellent!

spaceman	stupid (also space cadet)
spaced out	high on drugs
sparrer legs	thin legs
stoned	high on drugs (formerly drunk)
stash	(i) hide
	(ii) hidden goods, usually stolen
	(formerly a sailor's belongings)
straight (up)	honest, e.g. *straight, I didn't do it*
straightener	fight
sup	drink
sussed	found out
sussies	suspenders (now a rare sight,
	even down at the docks)
swipe	steal

T

ta	thanks
tabs	drugs
talent	attractive male or female (sometimes applied collectively)
ta-ra	goodbye
tattyhead	you
tear-arse	uncontrollable
tip	municipal rubbish dump
tizzie	over-excited
thingy	any person, place or object which does not immediately spring to mind
tod	alone
togga	football
tosh	mate (now obsolete)
tottie	girl, woman

took	spoken for
trabs	(see trainees)
trackies	tracksuit bottoms
trainees	trainers
two dogs fight'n	Huyton (a district of Liverpool)

U

ullo	how are you?
us	me

W

wack	mate (now obsolete)
wacker	(i) mate (now obsolete)
	(ii) humorous character (now obsolete)
wanna	would like to

wayo!	just a moment!
well away	becoming drunk
wet nellie	(i) cake, a Liverpool speciality
	(ii) weakling
whip	steal
wild	diarrhoea
woollyback	someone who isn't a Scouser
worra	what a, e.g. *worra lorra money*
worral	what will, e.g. *worral 'appen?*
wrecked	drunk

Y

yer	you
yer wha'?	pardon?
yew	you (accusingly)
yews	as above, plural
yerrokay!	for God's sake, shut up!

Z

zarrafact?	I don't believe you

PRONUNCIATION

The immediately recognisable features of the Scouse dialect are the congested, nasal sounds reminiscent of catarrh, together with a plaintive singsong pronunciation where a sentence starts with a slightly whining intonation, rises questioningly in mid-sentence, ending on a higher pitch.

Additional features include:
- An adenoidal tone where 't' and 'th' become 'd', or a 'd' is added: e.g. *id does or dthe boss*
- The ending '-y' (as in 'windy') becomes 'ee' and is pronounced with as much glee as the word itself, e.g. *worra classee tart!*. Since 'ee' does not feature in any of the dialects which neighbour Liverpool, before the Scouse Diaspora the extent of 'ee' marked the edge of the Scouse dialect area.
- Frequently mid-word vowels change sound (proper linguists call this the diphthong), adding to the lilting tone: e.g. *Mairy likes Tony Kairtis*
- The letters 'd' and 't' are aspirated into a lisping pronunciation with the addition of an 's': e.g. *dsrinkin' up time, Tsony*
- Where lazy southerners, especially on the BBC, omit the letter 't', Scouse substitutes an alternative, usually an 'r': e.g. *norra nother one!*
- Sometimes 'th' becomes a 'd' or 't' to show the Irish influence: e.g. *I wanted four, but dere's only tree*
- As in other dialects, a 't' ending is often omitted through laziness, but Scouse changes the 't' to 'tch': e.g. *play tightch up frontch*
- As with most dialects, the mediaeval Anglo-Saxon '-ing' word-end is usually dropped for the hasty 'n' instead: e.g. *I didn't do nutt'n*. With, of course, the obligatory double negative.

- The possessive 'its' becomes 's': e.g. *'s not mine*
- The letters 'l' and 'm' are often not allowed to nestle together undisturbed and so Scouse introduces a vowel: e.g. *there's a good fillum on telly*
- At the end of a word, the letter 'k' can slur into 'ch': e.g. *play tight at the bach*
- Recently, there has been a change in the Scouse diminutive with which the speaker speeds up sentences. Traditionally it meant changing the word ending to 'y' or 'ee'. Lately, the letter 'o' has been the substitute. There does not seem to be any grammatical rule to the construction of diminutive endings except that the shorter words mostly adopt 'ee' or 'y' while the longer words are shortened by 'o': e.g. Tommy Smith = *Smithy*, Phil Thompson = *Tommo*

- One aspect of Scouse which confuses the outside linguist is the co-existence of two different vowel sounds, best illustrated by the 'ur-air' difference. Before the great Scouse migration to other parts of Merseyside, there was a subtle nuance in the Scouse dialect between northern 'Bootle' and southern 'Toxteth' versions; this latter emerges in the John Lennon song:

> *And be-fore long I fell in luv with hur.*
> *Now I'll nevur dance with anuthur,*
> *Since I saw hur standin' thur.*

In the northern part closer to the docks and city centre, 'Bootle Scouse' is best illustrated by the well-known Ken Dodd line:

"Waair's mi shaairt?"

As a broad rule of thumb, the Scouse dialect becomes weaker with distance from the waterfront, although increased population movement within the city has complicated this somewhat oversimplified explanation.

• Finally, in the city's leafy suburbs and across the River Mersey on the Wirral, a softer dialect known as "Posh Scouse" exists, but no matter how hard they try, these sophisticates cannot shake off their origins.

IDIOMS

The city's docks, shipyards and merchant shipping have been a rich source of idiomatic speech.

Sling yer hook	Resign, clear off
On me hook	Out of work. (The docker's steel hook was an indispensable item and under certain circumstances was not required)
Golden nugget	Sunday overtime (much sought after extra pay not involving too much hard work)
Easy six	See golden nugget
Blowing for tugs	Panting, out of breath
Under the lamp	Paid less than the rate for the job

Two well-known Liverpool aphorisms:

1) *"Couldn't punch a hole in a wet Echo"*
   (local newspaper) = weakling
2) *Passenger:* *"Do you stop at the Adelphi?"*
   (Liverpool's most expensive hotel)
   Bus Conductor: *"What? On my wages?"*

The most admirable Scouse quality is the ability to quick-wittedly affix a nickname to someone, which exactly portrays that person's characteristic mannerisms:

Nervous balloon	The foreman who constantly appeals, *"Don't let me down, lads"*
Diesel fitter	The worker who keeps saying, *"Diesel fit this"* or *"Diesel fit that"*

Fog Horn	Big mouth
Good shepherd	Checker who always sends too many sheep into his wagon
Guy Fawkes	Someone who always says, *"This place needs blowing up"*
Merry Christmas	Always saying *"Many of 'em"*
Stanley Matthews	When lifting a packing case, a worker who always says, *"I'll take this corner"*
Surgeon	A good grafter
Tired solicitor	Always asleep on a (packing) case
Torchy	A worker who always steals batteries
Weightlifter	Docker who waits while somebody else lifts the packing case
Wonder boy	Always saying, *"I wonder what's in this case?"*

OTHER TITLES AVAILABLE

Language Glossaries

American English/English American
Australian English/English Australian
Irish English/English Irish
Gay Slang
Geordie English
Lancashire English
Rhyming Cockney Slang
Scouse English
Yiddish English/English Yiddish
Scottish English/English Scottish
Yorkshire English
Home Counties English
Playground Slang
Police Slang
Prison Slang
Hip Hop English
Rude Rhyming Slang
Military Slang
Cumbrian English

West Country English
London Taxi Driver Slang

History

The Death of Kings - A history of how
the Kings & Queens of England died

Who's Buried Where - Royal & famous
people's burial places

Literary Quiz & Puzzle Books

Jane Austen	Gilbert & Sullivan
Brontë Sisters	Thomas Hardy
Charles Dickens	Sherlock Holmes
	Shakespeare

Abson Books London

5 Sidney Square London E1 2EY
Tel 020 7790 4737 Fax 020 7790 7346
email absonbooks@aol.com
Web: www.absonbooks.co.uk